Misfortunate to Miss Fortunate

Tameka M. Williams

To my village,

Thank you with every fiber of my being. I can't imagine where I would be without you. Each of you has played a vital role in my life, and you've fulfilled it to the best of your ability.

To my children,

You mean the world to me and more. You've witnessed the pain, the growth, and the building of a solid foundation firsthand. You have been my motivation from the very beginning, even before I first held you. Keep climbing and believe in yourself as much as I believe in you. When you ask me if you're ready or if you can do it, my answer is always yes. You have been equipped with the tools to build whatever your heart desires. And remember, there will be times when you need to rebuild, and that's okay. You already have everything you need. Be intentional in your thinking, planning, and execution.

Contents

My Love

In the story of my life, marked by frequent moves and a void in how to establish and maintain healthy relationships, there was a special moment that sparkled like a precious jewel discovered in a beautiful field. Oddly, it happened on a chilly and dreary winter day, the type that calls out to those who are in search of something authentic but unable to find it.

During my childhood, I was quite reserved and didn't speak much. Despite being stubborn yet playful, I was often seen as an angry child due to the family conflicts and generational issues I faced. Feeling isolated and unable to confide in anyone, it was fate that brought me to my very first crush when I was just ten years old.

With the whole world ahead of me, like an unknown map ready to be explored, our paths crossed at a local corner store. In that moment, our eyes met and I was instantly captivated by him - a handsome brown-eyed cutie who was labeled as a "bad boy" who would later be recognized as one of the most notorious "bad boys" in our neighborhood and eventually the city. Little did I know that his presence in my life would have such a profound effect on my journey.

My family and I moved around quite a bit. From first to twelfth grade, I ended up attending a total of seven different schools. While residing in the Pullman area of Chicago, it was common for us to frequently visit my extended family in the Roseland neighborhood. It was during these visits that I would catch glimpses of my crush, as he happened to live just a few blocks away from them. Eventually, we ran into each other face to face.

The encounter was short. With no words exchanged, he kindly held the door open for me, my sister, and my cousin as we walked into the store as he was leaving. Yet, in that fleeting moment, my heart felt a sense of warmth and I found myself entranced by his gaze.

As the days went by, he was always on my mind. I couldn't help but bring him up in conversations with my sister and cousins, who never missed a chance to tease me about my crush on him. I used to ponder what he was up to and whether he ever thought of me.

When my parents split up, I discovered we were relocating to my crush's neighborhood and going to the same school - a bittersweet surprise! Thinking about it always brought back that first moment I saw him, making me smile so much my cheeks would ache a little.

I would eagerly look forward to encountering him at school, yet I had no idea which grade or class he belonged to until I coincidentally spotted him in the hallway during the breaks between classes. Although we didn't exchange words, our smiles spoke volumes. My stomach was filled with fluttering butterflies, and my heart raced with excitement, as I couldn't fathom the fact that I would have the opportunity to see his adorable face more frequently. And, of course, his captivating brown eyes never failed to mesmerize me.

For a few weeks, these silent exchanges continued until one day I was walking down the street around the corner from my house. He was standing outside his home, surrounded by kids playing catch, riding their bikes, and grown men shooting dice on the corner. The weather was crisp, as I recall wearing jeans and a light jacket.

It was the year 1992… Snoop Dogg's "Gin and Juice", Ice Cube's "It Was A Good Day", and Mary J. Blige's "Real Love" were in heavy rotation blasting from every stereo in the hood. The fashion trends included crop tops and baggy jeans for girls, oversized t-shirts paired with overalls for boys, and "Jodeci" boots for everyone. We spent our days playing with click clackers, poppers fireworks, and jumping double dutch, snacking on flaming hot cheetos, blue raspberry suckers, and pickles with a peppermint inside.

We believed we were so grown, having experienced being latchkey kids, taking public transportation alone in elementary school, mimicking our parents by cursing someone clean out, and sneaking off to steal kisses behind bushes. Boys would show interest by slapping girls on the butt, while girls pretended to play hard to get but also letting young boys get away with a free feel.

As my crush approached me, he asked me my name and where I was going. As I revealed that I was heading to my cousin's house, he joined me on the walk. He told me his name, who I would later affectionately refer to as Coco or "Boo". He began flirting with me while stating how fine I looked. It was at that moment I discovered that he was 12 years old in the seventh grade, while at the time I was 11 and in sixth grade. His words, behavior, and confidence indicated a level of maturity beyond his age, particularly street smarts. I realized that he was more advanced than me, making me feel nervous and inexperienced in comparison.

Ever since that moment, my infatuation for him grew stronger. His walk, his talk, his scent, and the way he looked at me ignited my pre-teen imagination, making me ponder the endless possibilities. I couldn't help but wonder if he was already taken, and if not, would he ever consider me as his girlfriend? However, my shyness held me back, leaving me clueless on how to even approach the topic.

As the days went by, we found ourselves engaging in more conversations in the hallway at school or on the street. It was a relief that our communication was no longer solely reliant on our smiles to understand each other's thoughts. Observing him, I noticed he never had a serious girlfriend, despite constantly being around others, flirting, and acting mannish. However, I still believed I had a chance with him. I failed to realize though that he would eventually leave the school since he was a year ahead of me and would soon be graduating.

Growing up in the world of street hustling became more evident in his demeanor as we continued to engage, making a future together seem unlikely, yet I couldn't help but wonder about the possibilities.

In 1993, I started high school at the same school Coco was supposed to be enrolled as a sophomore but he hardly attended classes. Occasionally, he would make an appearance but quickly lose interest and leave. It was a common sight to see him enter through the front entrance of the school only to exit from the back. Evidently, the allure of street life seemed more enticing and perhaps even necessary for him during that period.

I socialized with other boys of course and my first sexual encounter was with someone else at the age of 14, yet I maintained a close relationship with Coco and always felt a strong connection to him, despite us not being sexually involved at the time.

The moment I turned sixteen, Coco and I consummated our connection, coinciding with my breakup from my previous boyfriend. I told him about what happened and he would always tell me to pretty much stop dating these goofies and get with him, "a real nigga". Shortly after that conversation, he asked me to stop by his place that evening since no one would be there. Needless to say, I didn't need much convincing to accept his offer.

When I arrived at his house, he expressed genuine surprise, as he had doubted I would actually come. Coco understood my feelings for him, yet he respected my boundaries and knew I was different from other girls who were overly eager to please him.

His house was eerily quiet, lacking in furniture and essentials since he only used that particular location for eating and sleeping while dodging the authorities. Despite being young, he was deeply immersed in criminal activities, causing him to frequently skip school.

"Hey Boo." I affectionately called him.

With a big ass grin on his face, he took my hand and led me into the house, shutting the door as we made our way upstairs.

He complimented my outfit and appearance as I was wearing a navy blue long-sleeved shirt, Pelle Pelle jeans, and Lugz boots. My hair was styled in a neat french roll with hair hanging down in the back. I recall him looking quite laid-back in gym shoes, a white t-shirt, and jeans. Fixated solely on each other, I knew exactly why I was there. Being around him made me feel secure and protected. I had complete faith in him and was prepared to share my body with him.

He hugged me, expressing how happy he was to see me, and started kissing me. In a swift motion, he knelt down to untie my boots, enabling me to slip out of them effortlessly. Afterward, he stood up and unfastened my pants, pulling them down along with my panties until they reached my ankles. With a dresser conveniently positioned behind me, he lifted me by my waist and gently positioned me on top of it, allowing him to remove the rest of my clothes with ease. Although he was known for his dangerous lifestyle, he always showed me a softer side that excited me.

He proceeded to touch my thighs, parting my legs, and savoring what was in between. In moments of pause, he complimented its beauty and flavor. He had always boasted about what he would do to me if he ever got the chance, and now he was proving that he would indeed follow through with his words. Once he satisfied me, he then got up as if he was about to penetrate me, but soon became annoyed because it was clear he had lost his erection.

He stormed out of the room we were in, so I decided to follow him into another room. I whispered to him reassuringly, letting him know that everything was okay and that I would wait for him. In an attempt to arouse him, I started kissing his neck and engaging in some dirty talk.

This seemed to do the trick as he became aroused again. He took control, grabbing me assertively and leading me back into the room. He bent me over the dresser and entered me from behind. Remembering his preference for being told to go harder, I did just that, which excited him even more. That night, I felt a deep connection between us, believing it was sealed forever, or so I thought.

Throughout the evening, we talked and laughed, exceeding all my expectations. He was undeniably my "Boo", despite the absence of a formal label on our relationship. We both understood our significance in each other's lives.

Over the weeks, we were intimate multiple times, yet one instance stood out the most - the moment he made love to me. The intensity of his gaze during missionary position and the tenderness in his touch showed the strength of our connection and his love for me. Despite other girls, he only desired to be with me.

He was well aware of my standards and respected my boundaries, which seemed to intensify his desire for me. Although we weren't officially a couple, he started showing possessive behavior towards me. I vividly recall a time when my pager kept going off due to low battery while I was with him, and he became enraged and crossed a line with me. I made it very clear to him that he should never cross that boundary again, and he quickly corrected his behavior. Despite his tough exterior, he was incredibly gentle and loving towards me, and I cherished that. Our bond was evident to those who knew us, as they could see the immense respect and love we had for each other.

We had an understanding that worked for both of us and I had no complaints. Everything seemed to be working out until a heated argument between him and a friend during a dice game took a fatal turn in 1996. Coco had a tendency to explode in various situations, and this instance was no exception. He completely lost control, and typically when he would reach that point, there was no way to calm him down. As a consequence, he was given a lengthy prison sentence and wasn't released until 2015.

It was crazy how everything changed when this happened. I used to tell him everything - my thoughts, dreams, family problems, everything! Due to a single poor decision, he was now behind bars and I couldn't help but wonder about the potential impact on my/our lives during his absence.

Despite never ceasing to love him, life had to move forward for me. I eventually found love with someone else, started a family, and got married. While I wrote to Coco every week, I couldn't receive his letters due to my marital status. However, I always made sure to answer his calls, and we eagerly anticipated those conversations. Although my husband at the time knew of my friendship with Coco, I chose not to mention the extent of our regular communication to avoid making him feel uncomfortable.

As time went on, our bond stayed strong, but I started to see Coco as the one who slipped away. I came to terms with the fact that all we could share were letters and calls. I stopped longing for anything more with him because his choices made it clear we couldn't be together. As each holiday came and went, life transitions occurred, and the seasons shifted, time kept moving forward, leaving him behind. He had sacrificed his entire young adult life for a jumpsuit, and that was simply at the hands of him.

Time kept moving forward, and I found myself almost two decades into my marriage with three children; two in junior high and another in elementary school, while Coco was on the verge of being released from prison. During one of our phone conversations, he expressed his desire to claim me upon his release. Despite the difficulties in my marriage at the time, I understood that reconnecting with Coco would only bring chaos, considering his past involvement in criminal behavior. I had no desire to be entangled in that lifestyle. He was officially released in 2015, and we didn't really talk much until three years later at my cousin's funeral. Since our families were acquainted, I knew we would eventually cross paths.

As the memorial service came to a close, many attendees, including my then-husband, left the church, while some family members stayed behind. Walking towards my cousin's casket for a final goodbye, I crossed paths with Coco, who had just paid his respects. Memories of our first encounter at that corner store flooded back as we approached each other, my heart racing until we stood face to face. Pausing, we embraced, feeling as if we were the only ones in the chapel. I let out a satisfied sigh, to which he chuckled softly and whispered, "Don't start." I smiled and we then went our separate ways.

Despite the passage of time, our bond remained incredibly powerful, and it seemed as though Coco had so much more to express. However, it was evident that the moment wasn't right for it. A part of me was curious to know, but I ultimately embraced the idea that whatever was left unsaid should perish alongside my cousin. Consequently, I didn't actively seek further communication with Coco.

As we were leaving the service, my cousin loudly said to me saying, "Meka, there goes Coco." She wasn't really known for being subtle, something that still makes me chuckle when I think about it now. I assured her we had already talked but Coco approached us and assertively claimed that I still loved him. When I asked him about his feelings, he confidently said, "I'm gonna love you forever. What, you thought I was scared to say it out loud?" I was completely taken aback by his declaration, but in that moment, I knew Coco and I would always have a special connection that would never fade away.

Sadly, in 2022, my uncle passed away, and Coco and I coincidentally met again during the repast and we found ourselves in another somber reunion. With a beaming smile on his face, I made my way towards him. It was apparent that he was happy to see me. He was holding two plates, a sign of his hearty appetite, and gestured for a hug by leaning in with his hands full.

This time, Coco didn't hold back and he opened up about his feelings, expressing the silent anger he held over the years towards me for getting married and starting a family. He wanted to know why I'd moved on and questioned whether there was a future for us as a couple. Despite knowing it wasn't possible due to his lifestyle, I reassured him he would always be special to me but we couldn't be together. Still, it gave me comfort to know that he never stopped loving me.

I could see he was upset, but we vowed to always be truthful with each other, and this situation was no different. Coco was undeniably my soulmate, but our destinies were never meant to converge the way he wished, and I believe he understood that deep down. In that instant, a strange sensation washed over me, as if we were genuinely bidding farewell to one another. I couldn't quite grasp it, but there was something distinct about that particular interaction, and it would take me just a little under two years to comprehend the reason behind that unexplainable feeling.

In the fall of 2023, my cousin called me about Coco. When I answered, I sensed something was wrong from her distant tone. She broke the news that he had passed away, leaving me stunned and speechless. It felt like time froze, and I was lost in my thoughts before bombarding her with questions in disbelief. Later on, she informed me that he had a heart attack. As soon as a single tear rolled down my cheek, I felt a flood of tears about to come. My heart shattered as he was truly my first love. I felt an immediate emptiness inside me and this time it wasn't a matter of him being in hiding or being imprisoned, but rather the fact that he was physically no longer here, and that fucked me up.

In the days before his service, everything felt incredibly unreal. He was constantly on my mind, and memories kept rushing back to me. I even wondered what would have happened if his life had taken a different turn, but then I realized that he wouldn't have been the same person I fell in love with. I went through a rollercoaster of emotions that I couldn't share with just anyone. I felt a profound sense of pain, and despite my best efforts, tears continued to flow uncontrollably.

I had mixed feelings as I prepared to bid my final farewell. The thought of attending his service kept wavering in my mind. I constantly questioned myself if I could handle it. There were moments when it seemed impossible, but I persevered because I needed to see with my own eyes that he was indeed gone. I got dressed, put on my makeup, and drove to the service alone, engulfed in silence. It was still hard to fathom that this was the end.

When I parked my car, I couldn't help but notice how packed it was outside, as he managed to gather the entire city, which wasn't surprising. As I made my way towards the entrance, I felt a knot forming in my stomach. I almost turned back, but I pushed through. As I greeted his family, tears were definitely shed. His uncle hugged me tightly and I burst into more tears. It was hard to believe that the last few times I saw Coco were at funerals, and now I was attending his own.

As his uncle guided me towards Coco's casket, I could feel my knees weakening and my body trembling uncontrollably. Anxiety engulfed me like a tidal wave, but his unwavering support helped me find my balance again.

Coco lay there, pristine in his all-black attire, resting on a soft silk pillow inside a glass casket adorned with an abundance of candles and flowers. It was evident that he was cherished by many, and I hoped he understood the depth of my love for him above all else.

Wiping away my tears, I prepared to walk away from him one final time, a smile appearing on my face as I recalled the first time I saw his stunning brown eyes. Despite everything he'd experienced, I found comfort in knowing he loved me just as much. In a soft whisper, I said, "Until we meet again Boo. I'll always love you."

Mama

Dear Mama,

I keep you in my happy place. When I look in the mirror, I'm blessed to see your face. Your beauty was more than skin deep. You had a heart of gold, making sure everyone was going to eat. You spent a lifetime caring for others—you were a girlfriend, mother, daughter, sister, auntie, cousin, niece, and grandmother. Most of all, you were a lover. A lover of all people, no one was above anyone in your eyes. To know you was to love you. It wasn't a disguise.

You were a whole vibe, accomplishing what most people failed at as they tried. A humble spirit, you didn't do a lot of talking. When it came to business, I admired how you walked it. You were a teacher. To some, you were a preacher. It took a special person to be able to reach her. When he needed guidance, it was information overload; you didn't skim. It took a special person to be able to reach him.

Your emotions got the best of you at times. You couldn't see through the pain; it had you partially blind. No matter what, you kept one eye open. When people thought you weren't listening, you were able to quote them. Word for word, sentence for sentence. They slept on you, Angel, assuming you weren't attentive.

I remember the day you schooled me on my name. It started out as the name of your childhood baby. "When I have a girl, I'm gonna name her Tameka Monique." Those words meant so much to me. Thank you for a name so special and unique. Love you beyond life, Tameka Monique.

Your transition was a huge loss. The game changer of game changers. Who would have thought? My babies loved Granny Angie. You had more patience with them than you ever had with your three. We're just grateful for the time we had. This chapter is dedicated to you, Angel, one of the most beautiful souls the world's ever had.

* * *

People often say those born on the 4th of July are determined and strong-willed, often doing good deeds in secret. That's me, Mama's Tameka Monique, born on Independence Day. I think parents have a special connection with their babies even before they are born, and because she knew me so well, she always made sure to celebrate my quiet but strong nature.

From the moment I came into this world, I had a heart murmur. Despite having a physical hole in my heart, Mama was there to fill the metaphorical void. She would brave the freezing winter and take me alone on the bus to see the heart specialist. Her love and care knew no bounds, and she made sure I got the necessary help.

At just seventeen years old, my mother became a parent to me. Despite her youth and the emotional baggage she carried, she managed to find enough love and care within herself to make sure I would be alright. The doctors informed her that if the hole in my heart didn't heal, I would have to undergo surgery. But Mama, regardless of the sacrifices, always made sure I never missed any of my appointments. She's always the first person that comes to mind when I think about what a real mother is like. She made sure my sisters and I were safe, taken care of, and didn't miss school. Her dedication to giving us every chance to succeed means the world to me and as a mother myself, I hold an even deeper appreciation, admiration, and respect for her.

Despite living separately from our dad for many years and not having a partner for support, Mama managed to provide us with a stable home and kept us connected with our extended family who frequently visited us or vice versa. Our home was always bustling with visitors and good times. As for my birthday, falling on a national holiday didn't stop her from making it all about me. Every year, she made sure we celebrated in a grand way, whether in our backyard, at the park, or on the beach. Mama always ensured that I felt special.

Of course, not every day was filled with roses and sunshine though. Mama had to confront her own past and emotional wounds that never fully healed, which influenced her perspective on life and her ability to trust others. I can vividly recall a time from my childhood when I needed assistance with fractions, but Mama struggled to understand how to help me. This led to frustration on her part, and instead of finding alternative ways to support me, she was unable to do so. There were moments when patience was a challenge for Mama, causing her to shut down and disregard my feelings and needs. As I grew older and gained a deeper understanding of life, I realized that her capacity to provide support in that particular area was limited. It simply wasn't her strong suit due to the trauma she had experienced.

During my childhood in the eighties, parents rarely discussed personal matters with their kids. It was clear that Mama had been through some tough times, but I never questioned her about it. Despite her own struggles and difficulties in providing emotional support or modeling healthy relationships, Mama maintained long-lasting relationships and was seen as a nurturer by her siblings and friends. My aunt even mentioned that Mama taught her how to be a woman, showcasing a close yet sometimes strained relationship between siblings.

When it comes to personal problems, I have vivid memories of my mother being frequently ill during my childhood. However, she rarely opened up about her health issues. Sometimes, it became a regular occurrence for me to return home from school and discover that Mama was admitted to the hospital. However, she always made sure to give us a call while she was there. It was always difficult for me to adjust because I never knew when she would return home until she actually walked through the door. Sometimes she would mention having a fever, while other times it was stomach aches. However, the true cause of her ailments remained a mystery to most of us. Additionally, my mother had trust issues, which made it challenging for her to let people get close to her in that way.

Mama spent several days in the hospital, sometimes up to a week, which always made me anxious. Despite my worries, she always managed to come back home. That's just how Mama was - she always found a way to pull through. I know she fought hard during those hospital stays to be with us again. But Mama was also very savvy too. She held down a job, and she also had side hustles that helped us live comfortably in the 'hood. She was great at talking her way through things and getting shit done. No excuses, just action. I think I picked up that trait from her.

Mama's emotions overwhelmed her as she struggled with her health. It was painful to witness, but I eventually understood why she acted that way. Although Mama was never clinically diagnosed with depression, there were often signs of it, despite her ability to manage our household. She managed to conceal it for a limited time, and I can only speculate about the burden she bore all by herself as a result. I really wish she had allowed someone to support her in the way she needed, but her past made it hard for her to be vulnerable in that way.

As time went by, I began to truly comprehend Mama on a deeper level. It meant everything to me when she embraced the role of a grandmother to my children. In her room, she had a special snack cabinet that we affectionately named "For You". Whenever Mama opened it, she would tell the kids to choose whatever they desired, emphasizing that it was specifically for them. Whenever my kids craved a snack, they would simply point at the cabinet and exclaim "For You". She had a unique way of being there for them, which I hadn't witnessed during my own childhood. Instead of dwelling on her weaknesses, I chose to appreciate and respect her for her strengths.

I was incredibly grateful that Mama expressed how proud she was of me. She mentioned that despite being a young mother, she initially believed I would rely on others to take care of my children. However, since I didn't, she was immensely proud of me. Hearing her say those words meant everything to me.

On April 3, 2006, I was on the way to a Chinese restaurant near Mama's place. While holding down a job driving a school bus and juggling college classes in between routes, my granny phoned me during my break to mention she hadn't heard from Mama in quite some time. I had a strange feeling that something wasn't quite right because I usually talked to Mama regularly.

My granny said it had been around a week since she last talked to her and insisted I check on her. I attempted to reach Mama that day but received no answer. I didn't manage to visit her house, but the very next day, everything took a turn for the worse.

Every time I entered the school, I never bothered to turn off my phone, but on that specific day, I did. Most of that day felt like a blur, but what stands out is the security guard and a family member walking towards me at school. Without uttering a single word, the expressions on their faces hinted that something was terribly wrong. A tinge of sadness could be seen in the security guard's expression as she stood there and my immediate question was, "It's Mama. Is she alive?" My relative confirmed with a simple "no."

I couldn't hear anything else that was said after that, but I distinctly remember sitting in my bus, sobbing uncontrollably and pounding on the steering wheel. The news had shattered my heart, and the thought of a world without Mama seemed unimaginable. I couldn't help but wonder what had happened to her and if she had suffered. Tears continued to stream down my face, causing my eyes to swell and making it difficult to see clearly. After a while, I gathered my composure and drove my bus back to the barn to pick up my car before driving straight to Mama's house.

When I arrived, a few family members were already there. Even though it was technically Spring, the weather was still chilly and I recall shivering a little bit from the cold. My uncle took charge and contacted the necessary authorities to conduct a wellness check on Mama, which confirmed that she had indeed passed away. Shortly after, Mama's lifeless body was carried out on a stretcher, covered by a white sheet. It was a sight that I couldn't comprehend. Mama was gone, and I was overwhelmed with a mix of emotions - disbelief, heartbreak, numbness, and even a strange sense of relief knowing that she would no longer suffer emotionally or physically.

I was at a loss for what to do when Mama was taken away in the ambulance, but I knew I had to divert my attention elsewhere to avoid breaking down completely. So, I decided to go ahead with coaching t-ball on my first day. By then, news of Mama's passing had spread, and some people questioned why I was even there. All I could explain was that I needed a different focus to cope with my grief. We all handle grief and loss differently, and this was my way of dealing with it. I had to not only deal with my own grief, but I had to support my kids dealing with the loss of their

Granny Angie as well. I couldn't even begin to imagine what lay ahead for all of us.

Mama wasn't for all the frills and extras. She had always been clear that she wanted to be cremated when she passed away, so we respected her wishes. Right away, my sisters and I started organizing her service, but honestly, I still don't remember much about that time. I was also comforting my kids and explaining death to them in a way they could grasp. It was hard as hell, and I was also dealing with a lot of emotions. I was grateful for the strong support I received from my church during that period, it made a huge difference. In the end, we opted for a simple memorial service, held just three days after she was found dead in her home.

The memorial took place at Gatlings Funeral Home in Chicago on a chilly day, lasting approximately two hours. Her urn was carefully positioned at the front of the chapel, accompanied by a large photo of herself on an easel surrounded by flowers. A popular Chicago singer, Dajae, graced Mama's service with a moving rendition of "His Eye is On the Sparrow". The atmosphere was heavy with sorrow and gloom, making it difficult to see any beauty on that day. My heart ached with a longing for Mama.

That evening, we all met up at my aunt's place and spent the rest of the day eating and drinking to cope with our emotions. Despite some moments of laughter, I couldn't shake off the overwhelming sadness that lingered throughout the day. Yet and still, I was determined to find a way to honor Mama's memory and ensure that she would always be remembered.

Mama, you were truly a gem and I will always cherish the memories. We will meet again Angel…

"In my father's house, are many mansions: if it were not so, I would have told you. I go to prepare a place for you. And if I go and prepare a place for you, I will come again, and receive you unto myself; that where I am, there ye may be also. And whither I go ye know, and the way ye know. Thomas saith unto him, Lord, we know not whither thou goest; and how can we know the way? Jesus saith unto him, I am the way, the truth, and the life: no man cometh unto the Father, but by me." ~ John 14:2-6

My First

I was filled with anxiety when I found out I was pregnant with you, considering my previous experience with a stillborn birth. However, as time passed, I prayed for your survival and thankfully, you made it. You came into this world during the beautiful season of Spring. I felt so fortunate and whenever I held you, I would sing to you. I even changed the lyrics to Maxwell's song, *Fortunate*, to fit my joy. Even after 25 years, right before I start singing happy birthday to you, I always sing that song. The memories of those moments still bring tears to my eyes.

As a child Jay, you were exceptional in many ways. You had a natural curiosity and mischievousness that set you apart. From flipping over the crib railing to getting a gallon of milk from the fridge on your own, and even climbing the neighbor's gate to jump on a trampoline at just three years old, you were always up for an adventure. Your first-grade teacher was unsure how to handle you because you were always the first to complete your work. Instead of staying quiet, you would often disturb other students by trying to help them. During your time in school, you participated in various extracurricular activities, such as baseball, basketball, football, and even helping out with the step dance team. You were unique because you also had the courage to stand up for yourself as the new student.

As time went on, you transformed into a tall, handsome young man with a brown complexion and a fit physique. Your confident stride and masculine voice, though not overly deep, added to your charm. Your well-groomed appearance and stylish caesar waves were always noticed and admired. You've always been one of a kind.

One day, my world took a drastic turn, and everything I knew was suddenly different. I still remember it very clearly. I was in bed feeling a little sick. I was trying to get some rest because later that day, I had to go to my friend's birthday party. It was early in the afternoon, and it was incredibly hot for a Labor Day weekend.

It was 2018, you were only nineteen years old and had a job at Speedway. Even though you were off that day, you seemed quieter than usual, giving off the impression that something was on your mind. Normally, you were quite silly and talkative, but I decided not to press you about it, as you, your brother and sister often told me I would be "doing too much" if I asked too many questions. Knowing that you were available and I needed to rest, I asked you to pick up your sister from work. After you returned, you left my car keys on the nightstand and told me you'd see me later and that you loved me. It was at that moment that everything shifted.

Later that day, T, your friend's mom, called me. We weren't super close, but we knew each other because her son, Ro always hung out at our house with you. I could tell something was wrong from her voice. Before I could ask, she told me that you called her to inform her that Ro had been shot. I screamed in shock. She also told me that you were on your way to the police station but she didn't know which one. I bombarded T with questions about when, where, and who, but she didn't answer them. She just reassured me that she knew you had nothing to do with it. That made me feel a little better, but I was still confused and worried. It was every mother's worst fear, and my heart went out to T, but I couldn't help but worry about you as well.

Your sister frantically called various police stations to locate you, while I was rushing to get dressed in the process. It was clear that you were with Ro when he got shot. Eventually, we found your location, but we couldn't see you because you were being questioned. You told T that Ro was being taken to Christ Hospital, so I decided to go visit T there. On my way there, I asked her if she had eaten anything, and she said no. I also offered to bring her some food, but she declined. I had to give it a shot though. Every time I thought about what T must have been going through, it just broke my heart.

Uugh, I hated hospitals. The constant sounds, from beeping monitors to the hum of medical equipment, creates a sense of urgency. Overhead announcements and the footsteps of staff added to the bustling environment. Conversations between doctors, nurses, and patients only heighten the anxiety and stress. The air was filled with the sterile smell of disinfectants and antiseptics. The clinical white walls, medical posters, and signage contributed to the overall sterile ambiance. Everywhere you look, there are sick and distressed patients in beds, doctors and nurses in scrubs, and worried visitors hoping for positive news about their loved ones. The chaos and intensity of emergency rooms and intensive care units can push anyone to their limits while they wait for updates.

As soon as I got to the hospital, I noticed detectives were there too, looking for answers. One of the officers came up to me and started asking questions when they discovered who I had come to visit. They mentioned that they were trying to find the family. T's eyes showed a pain that will always stay with me. It was clear she was struggling, clinging to hope for her son's survival. We sat together, watching her pace with worry. I wouldn't want anyone to experience that level of pain and anxiety.

Suddenly, the code blue alarm blared through the intercom nine times, indicating Ro's critical condition. T pleaded desperately with the doctors to save him, but his chances of survival were slim due to the severity of his injuries. Despite the doctors' efforts, the extent of the trauma left no room for a life-saving surgery, and he passed away shortly after.

I quickly switched into helping mode and took T's younger set of twins, who were four years old, downstairs to get them something to eat. Meanwhile, the rest of the family stayed upstairs, processing the news of Ro's death. I stayed with the twins, keeping a close eye on them and keeping them occupied. Eventually, we tried to go back upstairs, but security didn't allow it. As I was preparing to leave to see you at the police station, T's older set of twins came downstairs. I attempted to give them the food they had requested earlier, but by then, they had lost their appetite.

In the hospital parking lot, I caught sight of a few friends of yours and Ro. They seemed engrossed in their phones, watching a video captured by someone's security camera, which revealed the murderer running. It seemed that someone had recorded it and now it was being shared among friends.

One of them mentioned that a guy in the video was the killer, but I didn't recognize him, nor did I see you, Jay.

Once I left the hospital, I reached out to a lawyer who then contacted the police station seeking answers. However, the police insisted that the lawyer had to be physically present. When I finally arrived at the police station to meet you, they denied my request to see you because you were not a minor. I questioned why you hadn't contacted your family yet, and was told you didn't request a phone call, which struck me as strange. Feeling helpless, I had no choice but to return home. It felt like the longest night of my life, knowing you were in a jail cell and I couldn't do anything to help. I couldn't sleep, eat, or focus on anything else, consumed with worry about your well-being. My mind was filled with wild thoughts of you, covered in blood and completely distraught while holding Ro. However, reality proved me wrong as none of that was true.

I couldn't see you on the second day because you were still being questioned, and on the third day, you were charged. I felt the wind leave my body - you were accused of committing a first degree felony murder! I was in complete disbelief. You were my precious child, the one I used to sing to all the time when you were little, and now they were charging YOU with murder? Seriously, what the fuck? It hadn't even been 72 hours since the incident, and they had already slapped you with the harshest punishment, despite your clean record. It just felt incredibly unjust.

I found out later that Ro tried to rob the local weed dealer, and everything escalated quickly. When he got shot, you stayed by his side and called for assistance. However, you also voluntarily went in for questioning because you were unaware of your rights and believed you would leave the station without any consequences. Little did you know, the police coerced the killer into corroborating the story.

It was disturbing to see the police manipulate evidence and pressure someone into confirming a story just to make charges stick after watching hours of investigation footage. The murderer lied for quite some time and the police provided the information.

The murderer asked how much time he would have to do, to which the police informed him you were in the other room and said they knew everything. However, he was ultimately released on the grounds of self-defense. Feeling unconcerned, he pretty much enjoyed his meal from

McDonald's and peed in a cup while waiting for the detectives to return. When they did, they showed him a still image of himself but refused to show him the actual footage. After hours of intense questioning, I witnessed your breaking point when the detective slammed the table and declared that Ro was dead. You were in a state of shock and disbelief, repeatedly asking if he was still breathing. In that moment, I saw your life change. From a young age, I instilled in you and your siblings the belief that your mind is your most powerful weapon. After all, everything begins as a mere thought but learning about Ro's death in that way shattered you.

The pain from grief was overwhelming. Eating and sleeping became difficult for me, yet I needed to remain strong for you and your siblings. The idea of you not being able to find closure by bidding farewell to Ro pained me deeply. Over the years, thoughts of you losing loved ones, friends, and your father and I divorcing weighed heavily on me as the family gathered, leaving you alone with only prison walls. I always warned you to stay out of trouble because I couldn't afford legal representation. I mentioned you would have to face the consequences alone, until that first call came from you after you were charged.

"Hey Ma. Are you going to be in court tomorrow? Do you know what they charged me with?"

The mixture of anxiety and innocence in your voice cut me to the core. I prayed for you and assured you that I would support you through it all. Seeing you struggle made me reconsider my stance on not being able to afford a lawyer. I couldn't stand by and watch the system take advantage of you. I couldn't bear the thought of you missing out on important moments like birthdays, holidays, family gatherings, and vacations.

I found myself in a tough spot when you, Jay, my boy, were facing jail time and I didn't have any bail money to help you out. Just a year after finishing high school and taking college courses, this was your reality - a harsh one. The days turned into years, with court dates dragging on for five and a half years until your sentencing in July 2023. Throughout this ordeal, Ro's family's attitude towards you shifted, as if they forgot the kind and loving person you were. I could see the pain in your eyes and the reluctance to speak up during your sentencing, especially after Ro's sister expressed not caring about what happened to you.

Despite the challenges, I always made sure to visit Cook County Jail without fail. I recall a time when my flight got canceled in Texas due to bad weather, leaving me stranded. Determined not to miss seeing you, we rented a car, drove through the night, and arrived just in time with only five minutes to spare before visitor hours ended. The 16-hour drive was exhausting, but it was all worth it to be there for my boy.

I make an effort to come and see you once a month. I rent a car, book a hotel, feed you, and make sure I spend enough time with you so you know I haven't forgotten about you.

Despite your new address, you continue to show empathy towards others. You recognize the significance of having someone by your side during these difficult times. Whenever people around you receive distressing news or when special occasions like holidays or birthdays arise, you reach out to me and request that I provide them with words of encouragement. Throughout the years, I have sung happy birthday to numerous men to bring a moment of brightness to their day. As a parent, I take my role seriously and understand the importance of my responsibilities. We eagerly anticipate your return and believe that you will accomplish remarkable things when you are released. I am confident that this experience will enable you to assist other families in a meaningful way.

Even though you were given a 15-year sentence with a 50% reduction, my love for you remains strong and will never waver. Our bond cannot be broken by any jail cell, and I will always be there for you, guiding you through the toughest moments. Jay, I love you and I will always remain strong for you.

My Angels

Takiya

Valentine's Day is typically associated with love, romance, and showing appreciation for loved ones, whether they are romantic partners, friends, or family members. However, it can also be seen as a commercialized holiday driven by consumerism, with businesses promoting gift-giving. In different cultures, the significance of Valentine's Day may vary based on historical or religious traditions. But for me, since 2017, Valentine's Day has never been the same.

When February comes around, I can feel the impact of post-traumatic stress on my body. I often struggle with loss of appetite, focus, and sleep, in addition to feeling stressed out. Sometimes, I get really angry and end up crying uncontrollably because it's hard to accept that such a young girl was taken from us. Takiya was a sweet innocent angel with her whole life ahead of her who didn't deserve this. I vividly recall the day after she was shot, when I had to leave work early due to the knots in my stomach and constant tears. I was so devastated and enraged that I almost punched the window out of my car on the way to the hospital. I screamed, "She's just a baby!" The shock of that time still haunts me as a complete nightmare.

Takiya was the only child of my first cousin. We were raised like siblings and have always been there for each other, so seeing the pain my cousin went through was incredibly difficult. Takiya was a sweet, fun-loving child. She was involved in an African American cultural group, soaking up knowledge about the culture. She was only 11 years old and I can't help but think about what her life could have been like if she had the chance to live it. While many of her peers were getting ready for prom this year, it would have been really special to see her experience that important cultural milestone that we usually celebrate. Her passing is still something I can't wrap my head around, even now.

Takiya got caught in a crossfire on February 11, 2017, and was shot in her mother's minivan in the Parkway Gardens neighborhood. I had just returned home after celebrating Valentine's Day on a Saturday, since it happened to fall on a Tuesday that year. My dad called me that same evening to deliver the devastating news. Takiya was rushed to Comer Children's Hospital, prompting my family and me to quickly head there. I visited her for two consecutive days after work, and on February 13 th, I went again to pray and talk to her while she was connected to a machine. Despite her lack of response, I had faith that she could hear me.

On February 14th, I woke up to the breaking news that Takiya had been taken off life support and had passed away. The pain my family felt was unbearable, and when we gathered to honor her life, the church was filled with news reporters and emotional children speaking about how much they would miss her. It was truly heartbreaking to hear their tributes and see the tears they shed. Takiya looked so beautiful and precious, resting peacefully in a white casket. However, the thought of her funeral being broadcasted on the news and seeing her carried out in a casket really hit different for me.

It's been nearly seven and a half years since Takiya was taken from us as her murderer was recently sentenced to 71 years in prison on February 6, 2024. Even though justice was served, we can never bring Takiya back. There's no right way to deal with that kind of pain except to hold onto the memories.

Lexi

On July 27, 2021, my 19-year-old cousin, Alexis (Lexi) Celestine Wilson, was killed by the Dolton Police. It's been heartbreaking to see my family relive the trauma of her unnecessary death without justice. As a parent, I can't even imagine losing a child, especially at the hands of those who are supposed to serve and protect us.

My family and I are still deeply upset by the anger we hold. I can't believe that so-called police officers would think it's okay to unjustly harm a young woman. It's unacceptable. Don't they have mothers? Grandmothers? Sisters? Aunts? Hell, any women in their lives? It's sickening to even think about! Dealing with grief is already hard without having to face injustice on top of it. I've watched the body cam footage so many times, it's crazy. I know it's not good for my mental health, but I can't help but keep watching in hopes of finding the truth.

The media is such a fucking joke. The coverage of Lexi's death and the misleading angles in the video on the news caused a lot of problems for my family while dealing with this case. It's caused a lot of division and confusion among the public and dealing with a high-profile case has brought a lot of pressure due to the intense scrutiny involved. However, there have been people who have offered their support, prayers, and push for justice and accountability.

Dealing with this situation has led to major legal and financial difficulties as well, taking a toll on my family emotionally and financially. It has also further strained the relationship my family and I have with law enforcement and the justice system. The repercussions of that night when Lexi was taken away from us have been significant, and it frustrates me that the officer didn't consider the consequences of shooting and killing my cousin before pulling the trigger.

I'm still so angry about everything that's happened. It's completely unjust, and I can't pretend to accept losing Lexi the way we did. She should still be here, working towards her academic and career goals, spending time with loved ones, and figuring out her future.

Saying goodbye to Lexi at the church was filled with so much pain. It was overwhelming, as the atmosphere was thick with grief, making the air feel dense and heavy. Emotionally, there was a deep, pervasive sorrow that led to many tears, a sense of emptiness, and an immense feeling of loss. People found it hard to speak, caught between the desire to express their grief and the fear of breaking down. It was a collective sadness that penetrated the service, creating a shared, noticeable sense of mourning.

The pain was both personal and communal. Individually, each person grappled with their unique memories and loss, while collectively, there was a shared acknowledgment of Lexi's impact on everyone present. This duality made the pain feel both isolating and unifying. Watching Lexi being laid to rest, placed in a horse and carriage, was bittersweet. We would all miss her, but witnessing her being sent off in such a beautiful way brought a sense of comfort amidst the sadness.

Dear Angels,

You will forever be missed. The potential for you to change the world has been taken away, and I'm pissed. The void in life can never be filled. For those who don't understand, this pain is real. Looking into your parents' faces and seeing their grief, I wish there was something I could do or say. Whatever is asked of me, I won't hesitate.

What is justice today? Locking a murderer away won't bring you back, angels. Sometimes I get so upset, I don't know what to do. I know what I want to do, but causing more pain to the family means we all lose.

What is justice today? Being protected by a badge and other crooks, making it okay. Last I checked, murder was a crime. I guess it depends. For you, the system goes blind. But blindness can be temporary. I'm rooting for Tee Tee. Let justice be served for Lexi!

To my cousins,

I love you beyond words. Our angels will never be forgotten. They knew they were loved while they were here. Being a parent is everything but easy.

Fuck COVID

At the start of the COVID-19 outbreak in the United States, there was a lot of confusion, uncertainty, and information that kept changing quickly. The initial case in the United States was documented on January 21, 2020, in Washington state. The person had just come back from Wuhan, China, where the virus started spreading. At first, COVID-19 was mostly linked to cases from traveling. But then, it started spreading within communities. The U.S. government put travel limits on China on January 31, 2020, and later added more countries to the list.

Initially, a lot of people didn't take the virus spreading seriously. Some, like me, believed it would just go away on its own and not impact us personally. We couldn't have been any more wrong. People started to pay more attention and worry as more cases of the virus were reported, especially in Italy and Iran. Confusion among the public was caused by false information and conflicting messages from different sources. Before we knew it, by mid-March, local and state governments started telling people to stay at home, closing schools, and shutting down non-essential businesses. The federal government said it was a national emergency on March 13, 2020. All I could think to myself was, *"It's getting real now."*

Hospitals and doctors didn't have enough masks, gloves, and other important gear. They also didn't have many ventilators and other supplies they needed. At first, they couldn't test many people for the virus, which made it hard to stop it from spreading. The societal impact was crazy! The stock market went up and down a lot, especially the Dow Jones Industrial Average which experienced sharp declines. Many people lost their jobs because businesses closed or cut back. In March, the CARES Act was passed to provide economic relief.

Social distancing rules were put in place, and phrases like "flatten the curve" became popular. People started working from home and attending virtual classes. Many events and gatherings were either canceled or rescheduled. Stores experienced high demand for items such as toilet paper, hand sanitizer, and non-perishable foods, causing temporary shortages on their shelves.

At first, the CDC and WHO did not recommend mask-wearing for the general public, only healthcare workers. That later changed as evidence of asymptomatic spread was found. I found it strange that they were highlighting frequent handwashing, hand sanitizer use, and keeping a physical distance from others as important prevention measures, as I thought these were things we should already be doing regularly.

During the early months of the pandemic in the United States were characterized by rapid changes, significant societal disruptions, and a growing realization of the virus's severity and long-term impact. It was a shit show, to put it simply, and I found myself right in the thick of it as an essential worker. At that time, I worked as a home-based therapist for an agency that had a contract with the Department of Children and Family Services. During the stay-at-home order, I received a letter from the governor to show to authorities in case I was stopped while outside. What a time it was to be alive, both figuratively and literally.

Working as an essential worker was a frightening experience for me and my family. The uncertainty of returning home safely each night weighed heavily on my mind, but I tried to stay positive to shield my children from worry. I witnessed the fear in people's eyes as they anxiously followed the news for the latest death toll updates. Many healthcare professionals, including doctors and nurses, resigned due to the overwhelming trauma they faced. The hospitals were overwhelmed with the number of deceased individuals, leading to the use of mobile freezers outside the facilities.

Despite all the chaos that was happening during that time, what really hit me hard is how COVID impacted me personally. It felt like a sudden intrusion, snatching away some of my loved ones. So yeah, I'll keep saying fuck COVID every damn day.

My paternal grandfather, Sunny, left me with countless cherished memories. He was the only grandfather I knew, as my maternal grandfather passed away before I was born. As a child, I remember him strolling around the neighborhood, planting fruits and vegetables. He was the one who first introduced me to fried frog legs, which I still enjoy today. He would always shout to his grandkids, "Hey, you bangies!" We never really understood where it came from or what it meant, but he said it with so much affection that we just took it as a term of endearment and never asked him about it. His love for his grandchildren was always evident.

Unfortunately, he contracted COVID while living in a nursing home. I couldn't visit him due to restrictions, but my dad was by his side throughout his battle with the virus, which brought me some comfort. However, COVID's impact didn't stop there, spreading like a destructive storm through my family.

Big Rob, also known as Big Baby, was my cousin who was fun-loving, family oriented, and had absolutely no filter. His hugs were the biggest and the best, capable of making anyone feel better, even if just for a moment in his arms. He was the spitting image of his father, my Uncle Robert, with a smile that could light up the whole city, making him well-known to many.

Big Baby and I drifted apart during our childhood, and I'm not exactly sure why. It could be because he had a different mother than his siblings, and his mother may not have been close with the family. However, it was great when we reconnected later in life. We always enjoyed spending time together, talking about anything and everything without holding back. Sometimes, I'd be shocked by his blunt and unfiltered comments, making my eyes bulge out of my head. But that was Big Baby, as real and genuine as they come.

One moment we were laughing and having fun, then COVID came and changed everything. Big Baby was hospitalized for breathing issues, put on oxygen, and sadly, he passed away not long after.

Our family and friends experienced deep sadness when Big Baby passed away, with the pandemic making it even more difficult as traditional mourning practices were affected. Rather than a traditional memorial service, a balloon release ceremony was organized to honor him, followed by a gathering of friends and family for a neighborhood motorcycle ride in his memory. He had a passion for riding his motorcycle across different states and was actively involved in various bike clubs.

Big Baby's death also increased concerns about the virus and its effects on everyone, adding to the anxiety about our own health and safety. It led many to reflect on life's fragility, prompting changes in priorities, lifestyle, and relationships. The complexities of grieving during the pandemic were unique for everyone, leading to a divided world as each person navigated their own journey through the process.

COVID caused a great deal of unpredictability since it was impossible to foresee who would be affected next. My girl, CB also known as Granny C, was a 4ft tall, white woman from West Virginia with a third grade education. She couldn't go to school and had to work to help take care of her family as her father struggled with alcoholism. At the age of 13, Granny C moved out of her home to stay with her sister. After leaving her sister's home, she went to Detroit where she met a musician who later became the father of my eldest two uncles.

Granny and her family moved from Detroit to Illinois. She got a job at a club in downtown Chicago where her man was a member of a band. Since CB was not an acceptable name at the time, she had to choose the name Carol Beverly. Eventually, she sent her man back to Detroit and met my grandfather, Roy Lee Williams. Unfortunately, Roy Lee passed away before I was born. After discovering that she was in a relationship with a black man, Granny's family disowned her. Granny remained estranged from her family for the rest of her life. She was a strong, hard-working, loving, no nonsense person who spoke her mind all the time. Whether you agreed with her or not, Granny was always willing to go above and beyond for her loved ones.

One of Granny's favorite places to travel was Vegas. I used to tease her about how often she went there, saying it was her second home. After the restrictions were lifted post 9/11, Granny wasted no time and caught the first thing smoking on a flight to Vegas by herself. She was self-sufficient and didn't depend on anyone when she had to get from place to place.

Granny fell sick in January 2021. I remember it well because it happened around the time of my aunt and cousin's annual birthday trip to Colorado. A couple of days before we left, we spoke to Granny as she stated she wasn't feeling too well. While we were in Colorado, Granny called saying she wasn't feeling any better so my daughter and cousin drove her to the emergency room. It was difficult to hear the hurt in her voice. The medical staff provided us with the daily updates. My aunt inquired about Granny's health, to which I reassured her that Granny is resilient and will pull through.

Two days after we returned home from Colorado, the hospital informed us that the hospital only allowed two visitors at a time. I drove my aunt to meet my uncle there, but unfortunately, she passed away before we made it to the hospital.

My son, Jay, had a video call with Granny just a few days before our trip. We knew that he would take the loss pretty hard so we were unsure of how and when to tell him about her passing, so we didn't say anything during our conversations with him. Eventually, he asked about Granny, and I had to break the news to him. It was tough to hear the hurt in his voice after receiving the breaking news, especially since they were so close and he had already experienced another loss. He said that he felt something wasn't right but couldn't put his finger on it.

The dinner was open to everyone, but out of respect for Granny, some relatives did not attend her memorial dinner. Granny specifically said. *"When I die I don't want a funeral. I don't want all them phony muthafuckers standing over me crying. If they didn't give me my flowers while I'm here, then fuck them."* Saying goodbye to loved ones is tough as it is, but even harder when you can't have closure.

Following all that, I became very cautious as loved ones fell ill, and I ended up in a familiar scenario regarding my father upon returning from a trip. He called me the day before, requesting items from the store as he was feeling sick. When I returned, I rushed to Walmart, confirming with him over the phone if I had everything he needed. He mentioned feeling like he needed to go to the hospital. My aunt and cousin later informed me that he might have contracted COVID.

I arranged an Uber for him and waited outside his house so that I could follow the car to the hospital. He was in terrible condition. Considering my dad was one of the healthiest people I knew, it was shocking to see him so sick. I sat there at the hospital, feeling extremely anxious, thinking he's my only living parent. I've lost so many people. Please don't take him now, God. He actually tested positive for COVID and was hospitalized. I called every day for news until he was discharged.

COVID continues to affect people in several ways. The pandemic has led to increased rates of anxiety, depression, and other mental health issues due to factors like isolation, stress, and grief. And don't get me started on the healthcare system, work environments, and education. Hospitals and healthcare providers face ongoing pressure from treating COVID patients, managing long COVID cases, and addressing healthcare backlogs from the pandemic. Many workplaces have adopted hybrid or remote work models. Some sectors, particularly those dependent on in-person interaction, continue to experience labor shortages and financial challenges. Schools and universities have had to adapt to new teaching methods, including online and hybrid learning models. Students face educational disruptions and learning loss.

In the school system, children and families are struggling to readjust to being back in the classroom. Kids have developed habits that are hard to change. Working in the school setting, I've seen children getting overwhelmed by their classmates in a classroom and longing for a quieter, more comfortable environment where they can learn at their own speed. I could go on and on. Personally, I try to maintain some sense of normalcy for myself through gratitude and self-care. COVID truly turned my life upside down in more ways than one but I continue to focus on the present moment while remembering those I've lost due to this devastating virus. So yeah… Fuck COVID.

The "Me" in Meka

Throughout my life, I've faced plenty of criticism and lack of understanding, but I believe it's common when you keep your emotions guarded. People often mistake my tough exterior for who I am, without truly knowing me. I don't usually talk about personal stuff or share intimate details unless I trust you. I'm pretty strict about my boundaries, so I might come off as unapproachable or unfriendly sometimes.

Throughout my life, I've always been very independent, which has allowed me to handle challenges by myself. However, this independence might sometimes come across as arrogance or a lack of faith in others. I tend to observe my environment and people's actions before interacting, but this can be mistaken for being judgmental or overly critical. Due to my past experiences, I've learned to prioritize protecting myself and my loved ones, making it difficult for others to grasp my true motives and emotions, resulting in misunderstandings of my behavior and words. Don't get it twisted though. I won't apologize for being myself. My story belongs to me, and no one can change that.

I grew up as the eldest of three girls. For the first year and a half, I was an only child. I was mischievous and fun, and I spent my childhood surrounded by a gang of cousins. We shared some of the best years of our lives together, leaving little room for other friends. My parents were very protective. We weren't allowed to spend the night with relatives or friends in our early years, though we could visit often. Our cousins frequently stayed overnight at our home.

I attended Catholic school for first grade, and I went to seven different schools throughout elementary and high school. We moved around a lot, which made it hard to form long-term relationships until fourth grade. We grew up in "the hood," and the school-to-prison pipeline was a very real and pervasive issue in our community. I remember my eighth grade class trip to Cook County Jail, where we seventh and eighth graders toured the facility and walked inside a jail cell. What kind of message does that send to the youth?

Rehabilitated inmates spoke to us during the tour and even confronted certain students to scare them straight. My cousin was one of those students. I remember her crying as they yelled in her face, which made me furious. I started shouting, "Leave her alone! Get out of her face!" The teachers and staff calmed me down, explaining that they were trying to help her avoid making bad choices. Once again, what type of communication is this? It's hard to believe that these supposed "field trips" have actually made a difference when crime rates in underserved communities are still soaring.

I distinctly remember living in the inner city. I had a friend who would visit her grandmother on weekends. The grandmother lived across the hallway from us. My mother never allowed anyone but family into our home, so whenever my friend wanted to come inside, the answer was always no. As a child, I didn't notice the quality of furniture or other things in our house, but I knew our home looked different from my friend's. Once, we begged Mama to let her come inside, and Mama finally gave in. Shortly after the visit, there was a break-in. We had left to visit family, and when we returned, the door was open, items were missing, and our birds, Tweety and Sweety, were found butchered on the living room floor. That's when I understood why Mama didn't let just anyone into our house.

Living in our neighborhood often put us in frightening situations, but we always stuck together through it all. I remember a time when there was a shootout, and our building was caught in the crossfire. We were getting ready for bed, and I recall it was already dark outside. I was just thirteen years old back then. My mother yelled for us to get down, and my sister and I sat on the floor below the window in our bedroom, at the foot of the bed. A bullet came within an inch of the right side of my head. When it was all over, I got up and looked at the wall where the bullet had penetrated. I realized I could have died that night. It was clear to me that this situation was far from normal, yet it was the reality of the world we existed in.

There was another time when a gang war erupted, and men surrounded our building. I tried to run inside for safety, but a man wearing white gloves and pointing an assault rifle at my chest shook his head and directed me to go around the back of the building. There, other men with guns made me stand with them quietly until they were called off. The trauma of not knowing whether my loved ones would be murdered inside the building while I was outside was one of the worst feelings I could have experienced.

Once, I found myself in the local corner store when a robbery took place. My neighbor and I had just entered when a gunman walked in and ordered everyone to the floor. I was only eleven years old at the time. After taking what he wanted, the robber unmasked himself outside the store. As we passed by, he looked at me and mentioned he would have let me go if he knew I was inside. Although I didn't recognize him, he seemed familiar with my family. Seeing him around the neighborhood often made me fearful, especially considering what he'd done. And the fact that he was still walking around freely baffled me.

There was also a time at a house party, my peers and I were caught up in a police raid where we were all lined up against the wall. I quickly threw my pocket knife out the window to avoid the cops finding anything on me during their search. The person next to me discreetly moved a gun, which ended up near someone else. A young lady was taken away in tears in handcuffs for something she wasn't involved in. Everyone stayed silent, following the unspoken rule of "mind your own business."

Unfortunately, at a different neighborhood party, I bumped into an old elementary school friend. We chatted outside before I left, noticing the atmosphere shift as tensions rose among the crowd. The next day, I was shocked to hear that my friend had been murdered shortly after I left the party. I never knew what each day would bring. One morning, I woke up to the news that a familiar face had been brutally killed, with body parts strewn across the main street in my area. On a separate occasion, a young boy I knew met a tragic end inside a car parked right in front of my home.

One time, I completely lost it when we received a call about one of my cousins getting shot. We were practically siblings, so the idea of him dying made me a monster. All I wanted to know was what happened and who was responsible. I was side-eyeing everyone around him as I viewed them all as potential suspects.

Eventually, I became desensitized to it all. The constant exposure to violence and crime began to feel normal. The emotional numbness, changed perceptions of normalcy, the increased cynicism, heightened vigilance, reduced empathy, the impact on my mental health as well as the effect on my relationships with others started to become more prevalent.

And don't get me started on a car accident that nearly took my life. On my way to the penitentiary to see my uncle, RIP, Uncle D.S.H, I was in the passenger seat with my aunt driving. We stopped at a rest area before continuing. I remember the open road, cornfields, and no other cars. When we began driving again, I noticed something looked wet on the road, but not a puddle. Suddenly, my aunt screamed my name. I froze as the car spun out of control. I didn't want to see my death. The car flipped over into the cornfield and started sinking. We tried kicking and pushing the doors against the mud.

In the car was also my cousin, who was about two or three years old at the time, and she was nowhere to be seen. My aunt screamed, "My baby, my baby," thinking she had flown out of the car into the field. It turned out she was in the backseat, hidden under a bag filled with clothes. My sister was also stuck in the backseat, and it was difficult to get the seat up to free her. My aunt, with strength from the heavens, kicked and pulled until my sister was free. I can still hear my sister's voice saying, "Don't let me die." Once we were all out safely, we waited by the side of the road, watching the car sink deeper. With no cell phones, we had to wait for the next vehicle to pass, which seemed like forever.

While we were waiting for our neighbors to come pick us up, we received medical attention. When we finally went to check out the car, we were shocked by what we saw. The Toyota Celica convertible was completely totaled. Reflecting on the accident, we broke down as we couldn't believe we had escaped unharmed. It truly felt like a miracle that we only had minor scratches and no serious injuries.

Many of these situations just made me lose complete interest in a lot of things, including school. I just didn't care about much but shielding my family. Being the oldest, I became the protector, standing up for cousins and siblings. Many saw me as fearless with a strong sense of justice, unafraid to speak up against what I believed was wrong. I faced judgment on a regular basis because of it.

When I was older, I talked to my cousin and she told me she envied me when we were younger because boys and men always approached me instead of her. I didn't realize that some girls actually liked that kind of attention from men, I always shut it down. I never thought it was okay. I felt like I was always being objectified because of my looks and attitude. During my youth, I was a curvy girl with a light complexion, fine hair, and a jazzy attitude. I attracted a lot of attention from admirers, although often for the wrong reasons.

I vividly remember walking to my aunt's house on a hot summer day when a car pulled up alongside me. The man inside rolled down the window and asked, "Hey, are you fucking?" I crouched down, grabbed the biggest piece of concrete I could find, and replied, "Yeah, fucking crazy." He sped off immediately. Because I was different from the other children my age, I was allowed to spend more time around adults. I knew more and witnessed things that would have shocked other kids. I got my first car at 14, before I could even drive. I started my first job at 16 and left home at 17.

I talked to my mother about my plan to move out because I wanted to be independent and make my own rules. When she asked if I was sure, I assured her I was. My mother and grandmother found me a nice, affordable studio apartment, and my dad fully furnished it. My mother helped with groceries every month. While working and completing my senior year of high school, I attended all the senior events. Shortly after high school, I started a family. Once I became pregnant with my third child, I began to pursue my goals. Living in the hood numbed me for a long time, but I didn't want to be just another statistic, so I pulled myself together and worked towards getting my degree.

I started college when I was four months pregnant. Three days after delivering my little Christmas present in December 2003, in the middle of a winter storm, I went to school to take my final exam. I had even taken a few exams while in labor. My professor jokingly said my baby would be the smartest one in the nursery. When I returned for the final, he asked if we were still waiting for the baby, unaware that I had already delivered three days earlier. He mentioned he would have given me an incomplete until I was well enough to test, but I told him I didn't work that hard for an incomplete and wanted to finish the semester. I received an A on that final exam. I've had that level of determination since I was 17.

My mother died one month before I completed my associate degree. Despite the loss, I continued to pursue my bachelor's and then my master's degree, becoming the first college and graduate school graduate in my family. This includes my great-grandparents, grandparents, parents, aunts, uncles, first-generation cousins, and siblings. I made it my mission to encourage those who came after me to strive for higher education. I helped with college applications, financial aid forms, answered questions, researched and assisted with writing scholarship essays. I even took time after work to drive them to college and picked them up during school breaks. I say all this to show that I am a giver. When I win, we all win.

Even though I'm always ready to lend a hand, many people don't understand why I seem tough. If they knew the challenges I've overcome - from surviving a serious car crash to being in dangerous situations like a crossfire or armed robberies, witnessing crimes, losing loved ones, and more - they would view me in a different light. It's by the grace of God that I'm still here today, standing tall.

The loved ones I've lost would make anyone give up. I remember getting a call from my aunt in Iowa very late one night. I was nervous to answer, but I did anyway. She said, "Meka, girl, I tried calling your Daddy, but he's not answering. John called me and said somebody needs to check on Shawn. The house is on fire!" I was in a state of shock—thinking fire and no one's seen Shawn? This can't be happening.

I called my dad until he answered. He called back to say Shawn was dead and that he died from smoke inhalation. Shawn died just hours after his birthday. He was sitting in the upstairs bathroom on the couch and had fallen asleep with a lit cigarette in his hand. This was my uncle Shawn, my dad's youngest brother. When I was younger, he used to aggravate me endlessly by pinching my cheeks and kissing me all over my face while I tried to make him stop. It was the funniest thing to him. He would stand in my way and ask, "What's my name?" He'd say, "Say Shawnie Baby," and would repeat the same craziness every time he saw me. I couldn't believe he died the way that he did.

My final living grandparent was Bernice Armstrong, who was recognized for her time in the kitchen at Chicago Public Schools before advancing to an engineering position within CPS. Bernice, as the name she preferred to be called, was not old enough to be a grandmother when I was born. She was famous for hosting annual sleepovers for her grandchildren at her Roseland home, where we would watch movies, eat junk food, and use our Christmas coupons at McDonald's the next day. I remember her taking me and my siblings to Michigan, where she had a trailer for a few days. She also took us to Shaky's buffet. Bernice even pierced my ears when I was just a baby. I will always cherish the memories of her, but August 11, 2022 will always be unforgettable for me.

My aunt contacted me urgently about a family crisis involving my grandmother. She informed me that my uncle had been trying to get in touch with my grandmother for days without any luck. They were now at her house, with the fire department on standby to assist since my uncle's attempts to reach her had failed. After our conversation, I immediately called my dad, who mentioned he had heard from my uncle already and that he instructed my uncle to call the police.

As they were entering the house, my aunt called me back and sadly reported, "Oh God, she's deceased. I have to call you back." My dad rushed to the scene, only to find out that my grandmother had collapsed near the upstairs bathroom, where my Uncle Shawn had passed away years ago. The news of her passing hit me hard, especially knowing that she was alone at the time.

I had last spoken to my grandmother on July 31, 2022, when she mentioned she was heading to St. Louis, where she had another home, and planned to call me once she returned to Chicago so we could share a glass of wine together. It became apparent that her condition was more serious than we had realized. It seemed like she was aware of her impending transition and wanted to spend her final moments in the comfort of her Chicago home, which was her very first home where she raised her children.

I had four more hours left of my work shift and was trying my best to hold it all together. The memories of the first time I witnessed someone being taken out of their home on a gurney covered with a white sheet came flooding back. I was just a young child back then, about five or six years old standing outside with my family, witnessing the chaos around me as they brought out Ms. E, who had suffered a heart attack, from the same block where Bernice lived. Ms. E was the mother of my aunt's best friend (my aunt and her best friend babysat me together), who had a heart attack. The experience was so vivid in my mind, especially after seeing something similar after my mother's passing. Despite wanting to be with my family during that time, I decided against going over to the house after work, as I was not ready to relive those emotions again.

Bernice's passing was truly a shock to me, and the sadness of the situation was definitely visible during her funeral service among all who attended. As I approached her casket, the reality of her absence hit me like a ton of bricks, and I found myself struggling to catch my breath. The realization that her service was held in the same room where my mother's memorial took place added another layer of emotional weight to the already heavy atmosphere.

The memories of Bernice flooded my mind, and the thought of her no longer being around was difficult to process. She was the last living grandparent I had, and the plans we had to spend time together over a glass of wine seemed surreal. The shared sentiment of "damn Bernice" echoed in my mind, a sentiment that was shared by aunt, sister, and cousins whenever we mentioned her.

After the service, I found myself drawn to Bernice's home, where I spent countless days as a child. The nostalgia of the place, coupled with the absence of the familiar blue light bug zapper on her porch, made me long for the simpler times of my childhood. The memories of growing up surrounded by family on both my paternal and maternal sides, including our neighbor Turkey, who lived to be one hundred years old, added to the bittersweet feeling of loss. Again, all I could think to myself was, damn Bernice.

Four months later, Uncle Moe, also known as Jerry, passed away at home. The last time I saw him was at Bernice's funeral, and he didn't have a formal service, but friends and family could pay their respects at the funeral home for a couple of hours.

The scene was unlike anything I had ever witnessed before. Moe was lying on a metal slab, which I suspected was the same one used to store him in the freezer. He was wearing a jogging suit that my uncle had purchased for him and was covered with a floral blanket. The room was so cramped that it resembled a storage space, with as many chairs as could possibly fit inside. People who had known my father since his younger days came to visit, reminiscing about the things they used to do. Some of my father's friends even remembered me from when I was a little girl, although I couldn't recall them.

I couldn't stop thinking about who Uncle Moe really was. When he passed away, his wife didn't show up to see him, and no one pitched in for a decent funeral. I recall him and his wife bringing a spoiled chicken to a family gathering once. He was boisterous and had a laugh that could make anyone burst into laughter. Uncle Moe was the shortest of my dad's siblings, but he had the courage of a lion in the toughest of situations.

Six years ago, Uncle Moe made my birthday unforgettable by joining us at our favorite private lake with family from Michigan and Iowa. During a deep conversation, he surprised us all by confidently declaring, "They don't want to fuck with me," as he hopped up from his wheelchair on his one leg and thumped his chest. Uncle Ruthless, I mean Uncle Moe went out the way he lived. He never let his medical challenges, which resulted in the amputation of his leg, stop him from being who he was.

It's safe to say I've faced my fair share of challenges. The drive and resilience I possess have deep roots. My dedication to life, my loved ones, and the fight for social justice stem from my personal experiences. I see myself as a vessel with a clear purpose on this earth. If others can't grasp that, it's not my concern. I'll keep sharing my journey and living authentically as Tameka, unapologetically.

This Little Light of Mine (The Lessons and Blessings)

I constantly amaze myself with my resilience. How do you stand tall amidst storm after storm? This life isn't for the faint-hearted. A wise woman once told me, "Don't let it flood," when I mentioned how it seems to pour when it rains. From a young age, I felt out of place in the life I was surrounded by, even though it had its advantages. I knew I wanted to embody the nurturing, loving, and helping spirit I saw in my mother. She opened her heart and our home to family and friends, earning the title of "Mama" for a reason—the impact she had on their lives was truly remarkable. I wanted to be part of that, but on a larger scale.

My experiences have become a guide, enabling me to connect with those who view professionals as detached or lacking real-life experience. The lessons I've learned throughout my life have been invaluable. I learn something new every day. I pay close attention to what's left unsaid because that's where the raw, unfiltered truth often lies. Appreciating people while they're here has become deeply important to me. After all, what's the point of giving flowers once they're gone? I strongly believe in teaching people how to treat me as a way to build and maintain healthy relationships. My resilience is truly remarkable, if I do say so myself. When challenges arise, I remind myself that I've faced worse and come out stronger. The fact that I can still give, receive, and nurture soul-shaking love despite everything is a beautiful thing to witness.

For some, the shock will be real. Whether they interact with me daily or just a few times a week, most people have no idea what my life is really like outside of those moments. Self-care is essential for growth and freedom—it's like keeping a reserve tank full. I've learned that true happiness comes from within, and during my darkest times, when my silence spoke volumes, I had to draw from that reserve tank because no one else could heal my pain. I prayed, meditated, exercised, journaled, shared my experiences, faced my challenges, and lived with the mindset that this too shall pass.

I was taught there are four seasons, but I believe there are more: winter, spring, summer, fall, and the season of adjustment to any situation. I've found myself becoming and creating the change I want to see in the world. Today, I'm incredibly grateful for the lessons and blessings that have shaped me, making me appreciate every single curve along the way. Ha! I'm far from done learning and welcome knowledge with open arms. The process of introspection has been, to say the least, interesting—but the healing that comes from it is always worth it. Acceptance, courage, and the ability to sit with your struggles for as long as it takes to heal are everything. Walking in my truth and shedding unnecessary burdens is the path I've chosen.

I've broken unhealthy generational patterns and built a foundation so strong that, while it may shake at times, it's unbreakable. After everything I've been through, I still show up for "work" every day, wearing many different hats, with a smile fueled by gratitude and a glow that comes from the energy I've intentionally created. Bring it on, world—I'm always ready when life starts lifing.

To my readers,

Thank you for taking the time to journey with me through some of the toughest and most memorable moments of my life. This is a testament to the strength, courage, and resilience that some of the most influential people have had to harness to fuel their growth. But let's be clear—this isn't about "woe is me." Say it with me: Go Meka! Never give up.

I want you to understand that giving up is a personal choice. When the odds are stacked against you, remember to take care of yourself before making any decisions. You are enough, even when it doesn't feel like it. You can keep going, even when your tank is empty—build a reserve tank. When people leave, whether through death, incarceration, break-ups, or just walking away, make the adjustment. Sit with your feelings, give yourself grace, and figure out how the lessons and blessings can serve you. Surround yourself with love and people who genuinely want to see you thrive.

To the readers who may have formed a negative opinion, thank you for taking the time to journey through some of the toughest and most memorable moments of my life.

My love,

My love taught me not to settle for less than what I deserve. After over two decades apart, he came back and told me he would love me forever. He explained that the reason we weren't together and why he wasn't married to me was because I hurt him when I moved on, and he knew I wouldn't accept the games he played with others.

He went on to say, "You deserve better." When someone truly loves you, they respect you, see you, and appreciate you for who you are and what you mean to them. I am proud to have received the truest and purest love from my "thug love." He set the bar incredibly high, and for that, I will always challenge anyone whose words don't match their actions. Rest in Power, Boo.

Mama,

Mama taught me to prioritize taking care of myself before trying to care for others. She emphasized the importance of listening and seeing people for who they truly are, rather than judging them by appearances. She encouraged me to use the most powerful tool I possess—my mind—not just to look beautiful but to be beautiful. To turn my darkest moments into the sunshine I want to see.

As a parent, she taught me to be in tune with my children, to stand by them, love them, challenge them, and be their biggest cheerleader. To provide structure while allowing them to make friends and to make tough decisions when necessary, even if they don't like it. As they grow into young adulthood, I must trust that they have the skills to make informed choices and allow them to navigate their own paths, understanding the possible consequences.

As a partner, she taught me to understand my person and determine if they are right for me or just for everyone. To live by the golden rule, know my worth, and act accordingly. To persevere and take care of myself independently, while remaining open to a partnership without allowing anyone to control me with money or material things. Always strive to be the best version of myself, value education and stability, pay attention to my surroundings—especially the energy—and trust my intuition, no matter how convincing the defense may be.

My first,

No matter what I teach my children, they will grow up and make their own decisions, which will be shaped by their experiences while growing up. When they stray from the path, they will face the consequences of their actions. Eventually, the values and lessons instilled in them will become evident. Regardless of where they are or what they do, they will seek to demonstrate that the sacrifices, support, love, discipline, respect, and nurturing they received from me were not in vain.

Death,

Death has taught me to live each day as if tomorrow might not come. Embrace love, live fully, laugh heartily, teach with passion, show empathy, and make sure to appreciate those you care about while they're here. Be selfish when necessary—take time to unplug, regroup, and refill your reserve tank. Don't waste time worrying about others' opinions or those who don't see you for who you truly are. Focus on those who do recognize and value you. Manifest the things that elevate you and make your soul sing. Practice gratitude daily, and share your blessings in ways that allow you to multiply them and help those in need.

Who I am is who I was always meant to be; all the pieces fit perfectly where they belong. I often remind people that having a bad day is a choice. Waking up on the "wrong" side of the bed is just a phrase that people adopted without much thought. The fact that you woke up, have a bed, and can choose which side to get out of shows there's plenty of room for gratitude.

Dear self,

You are truly something special, and you never cease to amaze me. Your willingness and courage to reflect on the material in this book, knowing that there's so much more behind those experiences, is truly commendable. You had countless paths you could have taken, yet you chose to be responsible, refusing to blame anyone for who you are. Instead, you embraced the lessons and blessings, transforming them into something positive. You realized that your support system could only give what they had, and rather than letting that hold you back, you used the knowledge and skills you gained along the way to keep growing into adulthood. Life is far from perfect, but you navigate its challenges with grace. When others don't see or understand you, you recognize it's a reflection of them, not you. You're always willing to introduce—or even reintroduce—yourself to those who may have missed something.

There's always been something unique about you, almost as if you were touched by an angel. You've been protected from evils both seen and unseen, and in turn, you've touched so many lives. It's remarkable how someone might compliment something you have or are wearing, and without hesitation, you'll give it to them—simply to spread kindness and share the blessing. You never expect anything in return, just wanting to show that there are still generous and kind-hearted people in the world.

I remember a time when you were in the restroom at Texas Roadhouse, and a young lady told you, "You are so pretty." You responded with a heartfelt, "Thank you, and so are you." You took a moment to explain that beauty isn't just a physical attribute and that her ability to give a compliment was beautiful in itself. How many times have people trusted you with their lives, and each time, you showed up and never let them down? Now, the only direction is forward. Once again, you've turned tragedy into triumph and shared it with the world. I love you so much. Be proud of yourself.

With Unconditional Love,
Misfortunate to Miss Fortunate